Th
Guide to
Negotiation

Alexander Geisler

Oval Books

Published by Oval Books
5 St John's Buildings
Canterbury Crescent
London SW9 7QH
United Kingdom

Telephone: +44 (0)20 7733 8585
Fax: +44 (0)20 7733 8544
E-mail: info@ovalbooks.com
Web site: www.ovalbooks.com

Series Editor – Anne Tauté

Cover designer – Vicki Towers
Printer – J.H. Haynes Ltd
Producer – Oval Projects Ltd.

Cover image – © Photographer's Choice/Getty Images

The Bluffer's® Guides series is based
on an original idea by Peter Wolfe.

The Bluffer's Guide®, The Bluffer's Guides®,
Bluffer's®, and Bluff Your Way® are
Registered Trademarks.

ISBN-13: 978-1-906042-08-0
ISBN-10: 978-1-906042-08-X

CONTENTS

INTRODUCTION

Bluffing at negotiation is fun, easy and involves no sharp instruments.

Even as an apprentice negotiator you will meet many undemanding opportunities to bluff, and you would be well advised to master these before you are faced with the demanding ones. First, you must feign expertise in the subject matter of the negotiation. Would you negotiate the sale of submarines or the demarcation of international borders without suitable expertise? Of course you would, so long as you were able to bluff an appropriate level of intimacy.

Second, and even more important, is the pretence that you are a competent negotiator. To this end, you should adopt the air of one who has vast practical experience in the field. Practice by arguing over a parking ticket would qualify as suitable experience. Successfully talking your way out of one would fast track you to expert status.

> **You should adopt the air of one who has vast practical experience in the field. Practice by arguing over a parking ticket would qualify as suitable experience.**

The third tier of the bluff consists of whatever assertion, demand or bid you feel constrained to make – however outrageous. When shooting from the hip in this fashion, it is advisable to adopt a demeanour of calm assurance.

When staging this triple assault, remember that your counterpart is almost certainly doing exactly the same thing. Here lies the real structural integrity of the negotiation: two negotiators each indulging in their own triple-tiered bluff. Once you recognise that both sides are bluffing in almost every element of their presentations and that the entire process is a huge sham, you are well on the way to appreciating its merits.

THE PREPARATION

There are two very important words to remember about preparation: do some.

The main factors that will shape the negotiator's preparations are these:

1 Time is precious.
2 Negotiators are precious.

Negotiators consider themselves to be creative, even artistic. As a consequence, most do as little work as possible to prepare for the task. In fact many do nothing other than emphasise the need to prepare. This glib approach should be reserved for the advanced bluffer.

Given a choice between preparing the subject matter by studying it, or preparing a strategy, most negotiators are content to skip the subject matter. This frequently leads to negotiations where neither party knows much about what they are bargaining over, but each has a complex plan to ensure that they win. This usually works out remarkably well.

> **66 Given a choice between preparing the subject matter or preparing a strategy, most negotiators are content to skip the subject matter. 99**

Be wary of the dress code

In a negotiation, there are more than enough pitfalls that can lead to a debacle. Don't add to the list of perils before you have even left your bedroom.

If anyone can remember what you wore to the negotiation, you probably got this part badly wrong.

Consider the catering

The brain-fuel for those taking part is often given scant attention. Do not leave this vital aspect to chance, to others or, worst of all, to your opponent. Strict attention should be paid to the '20-minute' rule which is as follows. In any kind of negotiation that could last for 20 minutes, get the catering right and everything else will fall into place.

An all-day negotiation, for example, has to be preceded by a large cooked breakfast, in a small steamy café. A lunchtime negotiation calls for a goat cheese salad and a bottle of mineral water. A one-hour conference call on a Tuesday afternoon needs only a pot of tea and three Garibaldi biscuits.

Check the venue

There are only three things you need to know about the venue.

1 It doesn't matter where it is, so long you can find it.
2 It is worth investigating a possible means of escape. Marching purposefully into a stationery cupboard is not a good look. Similarly, if the venue is your own office, you will look preposterous if you walk out.
3 It is important to understand that those who claim to 'own the room' are not actually landlords. They are established negotiators who are just showing off.

We should add that the negotiator's fascination with 'Owning the Room' is overrated. Be quick to disparage the concept, even if you are not entirely sure what it means. It is advisable, but by no means essential, to offer an alternative. You will characterise this (along with any other theories you might advance) as the enlightened approach. 'Owning the Hedge' would fit the bill nicely.

It is extremely unlikely that you will be asked what 'Owning the Hedge' means, since the question would imply an embarrassing degree of ignorance. If challenged, improvise by describing a strategy where you take your decision 'out

> **Those who claim to 'own the room' are not actually landlords. They are established negotiators who are just showing off.**

of the room' (metaphorically) and hide it 'under the hedge' (even more metaphorically), in order to 'hedge' your position as the negotiation unfolds. 'Owning the Hedge' does not appear in any of the mainstream guides on negotiation, apart from this one.

Plan your image

Image is not everything – unless you have nothing else of substance, in which case it IS everything. You might imagine that if you know nothing about a subject there is no point pretending to be an expert. This is a logical enough proposition, provided you are a lightweight. The proficient negotiator would never be so reserved.

The truth is you have a choice. You can play the subject expert or the ignoramus. If in any doubt, do what all the other negotiators do: hold yourself out as an omniscient being, or at least a minor deity.

A good start is achieved if you can comport yourself with an air of serenity. If this is too demanding then at least try to reign in the nervous coughing and the more severe facial twitches. Confidence is the key. From the outset your opponent will be assessing you, trying to decide if you are a seasoned negotiator or a rank amateur. If you're going to bluff, you may as well bluff total expertise.

Research the opponent

If you can research your opponent before the negotiation, so much the better. Otherwise, do it when you meet. While your opponent is sizing you up, you should be doing likewise. This might be straightforward: if you are buying a second-hand car you will have a fair idea what to expect. If you are selling your house, you may have to make an instant appraisal.

> **While your opponent is sizing you up, you should be doing likewise.**

Know the subject

It is considered good form to know something about the subject matter of the negotiation. On the other hand most negotiators abstain from all forms of detailed research on the basis that too many facts might stifle their natural flair. This laudable incisiveness allows many negotiators to limit their research to one aspect of the subject – its value. This in turn enables them to confine their attention to one question; what's it worth?

Value is an irritatingly complicated concept, much trickier to understand than negotiation. For example, two identical houses can have different values simply because of their location. Unfortunately, you can't negotiate your way into a successful bargain without knowing the true value of each ingredient.

> **"Most negotiators abstain from all forms of detailed research on the basis that too many facts might stifle their natural flair."**

To make matters worse, 'value' should be distinguished from 'values'. Some of the most entertaining nonsense has been written on the subject of asserting 'values' and making 'value based propositions'. The trick is to pay scant attention to all this piffle and concentrate primarily on what the thing is worth.

Assemble your chips

Identifying, appraising and assembling the things you can offer is a critical part of planning. Negotiators get very excited if they can find something to offer that costs nothing but has a value to their counterpart. A good example of such a 'chip' is time. The ability to deliver part of a bargain quickly usually has a value, although there are occasions when proceeding slowly is more highly valued.

> **❝ Negotiators get very excited if they can find something to offer that costs nothing but has a value to their counterpart. ❞**

In considering the various elements that make up any deal, some will be under your control and others will not. It will make your life infinitely easier if you only attempt to negotiate the things you can control. You can refer to these as 'controllables'. (This is not a real word, so it has the added advantage that you can't miss-spell it.) It is surprising how many negotiators, veterans included, trade with chattels they don't own, money they can't raise and services they can't provide. You can promise that the sun will come up at midnight, but delivery will be tricky.

Have an end in mind

It's a good idea to have a vision of how the negotiation will end. To do so, ask yourself: How will I get there? How will it look? Will there be vodka and tonic? But there are other matters to consider first such as:

The maximum – Everything you'd like if your opponent is hapless enough to permit it.

The minimum – What you must have as a last resort if agreement is to be reached and your dignity preserved.

The reasonable range – A patch of land located between the above, where smart negotiators live.

The so called 'reasonable range' is important because most negotiations, when undertaken between two or more sentient beings, conclude in a deal being found within the reasonable range, or not at all. Indeed, for every variable part of every transaction, there will be a 'reasonable range'. Therefore it is not enough to identify the variables, you must also identify the 'reasonable range' of each. For example, before you call a plumber to deal with the lake that is submerging your lounge, you will have it in mind that 'next month' is not a time scale that falls within the 'reasonable range'.

> 66 Before you call a plumber to deal with the lake that is submerging your lounge, you will have it in mind that 'next month' is not a time scale that falls within the 'reasonable range'. 99

All this is part of having an end in mind. The trusted old adage for this goes as follows: 'Plan your negotiation and negotiate according to your plan.' There are two reasons why you might depart from this maxim:

1 You have never heard of it.
2 You have heard of it but you haven't made a plan.

A bluffer who falls into either of these categories should take a philosophical line (which is any line with the word philosophy in it) such as:

'My philosophy is to have an open mind.'

Have an open mind

You may have crafted a plan as to how the negotiation is going to end and how you are going to get there. If it becomes apparent that your opponent has done the same thing, then you have a simple choice. Nod understandingly or accuse him of being stubborn and inflexible.

> **"**Any notes (they don't have to be on the subject at hand) are valuable. They will give the perception that some preparation has been done.**"**

Suppose, on the other hand, that you have no clue as to what you are trying to achieve, let alone how. If so, you may legitimately claim that you have an open mind. Thus, your method is adaptable. This sort of approach will cause you to rely on your skills at improvisation and inventiveness. If you have no such skills then you may be in for a long afternoon.

Bring copious notes

Every negotiator knows the expression 'perception is reality' and some even know what it means. This probably explains why negotiators are fond of bringing notes to the negotiation. Any notes (they don't have to be on the subject at hand) are valuable. They will give the perception that some preparation has been done. In some circles large folded drawings can create a good impression.

> **66** Avoid the temptation to rummage in your notes for guidance, as you could lose focus and take your eyes off the table. **99**

However, it is imperative that whatever papers you take along, you should never look at them. Whether you have actually prepared or merely pretended to prepare is less important than whether you look as if you have prepared. At all costs avoid the temptation to rummage in your notes for guidance, as you could lose focus and take your eyes off the table. This will identify you as an amateur and, much worse, while you are distracted your opponent may tip pencil shavings into your tea.

A BEGINNING

Bluffers will be delighted to know that there is no predictable structure to a negotiation. Most veteran negotiators appreciate this although few would acknowledge it. Nonetheless, it is considered a good discipline to imagine that there will be a forseeable pattern, and to strategise accordingly.

It might be of passing interest to be able to recognise when the negotiation has commenced and indeed what to expect next. When events take an entirely different course, you can do what negotiators have done for centuries: improvise.

> **When events take an entirely different course, you can do what negotiators have done for centuries: improvise.**

If you come out of this experience in one piece, which you probably will, you may need to explain why your detailed plans were jettisoned. Put this down to a 'battleground decision' (a versatile phrase to which you should become wedded) or 'creative genius'. If at all possible, try not to admit to 'winging it' as this sort of talk can give the profession a bad name.

Posturing

The debutant negotiator may be a little surprised at how much time can be spent before anything meaningful takes place. This sort of naïvety is charming.

1 Initial posturing

It is never too early to commence posturing. As matters unfold your posture can be moderated or abandoned (after all, it's only a posture not a religious conviction). A good early posture to take is: Insistent but reasonable.

The bluffer will be cognisant that it is only a short step from here to: Insistent but unreasonable.

2 Negotiating the agenda

If someone has proposed an agenda, even if it is you, it is worth considering what to do with it. Generally speaking, negotiating the agenda is a worthwhile activity. Equally, for the more experienced or robust bluffer, refusing to negotiate the agenda should not be underestimated. Either way, you can gain valuable batting practice and an early

"As matters unfold your posture can be moderated or abandoned (after all, it's only a posture not a religious conviction)."

feel for the meeting, in the comfortable knowledge that subject matter is of no value whatsoever.

In order to head off the accusation that you are being deliberately pedantic, which of course you are, be prepared to justify this diversion on the basis that it is essential, either:

'In order to maintain a structure,' or

'So that we can use the time productively.'

Having interfered with the structure and used up copious amounts of time unproductively, the bluffer may care to chivvy the meeting along. This will demonstrate commanding management of the group. If you are being watched by clients describe this as 'meeting craft'.

> **Whether you have re-written the entire agenda or established that the original is sacrosanct, on no account should you adhere to it.**

Whether you have re-written the entire agenda or established that the original is sacrosanct, on no account should you adhere to it.

3 Establishing authority

Many an innocent negotiator has fallen victim to the error of deploying his full range of flamboyant bluffery to an opponent who has no authority to conclude a deal. The bluffer who discovers that his counterpart has to defer to someone else will have delivered a performance to the wrong audience.

> **It is well worth establishing that your opposite number has the mandate to be hoodwinked by you.**

So, before you indulge in your own shenanigans, it is well worth establishing that your opposite number has the mandate to be hoodwinked by you. The acronym of choice here is M.A.N. Be sure to negotiate with the M.A.N. because he (or, quite possibly, she) has the Money, Authority and Need.

4 Rhetoric

The subtle difference between rhetoric and utter codswallop depends only on the context. In dignified negotiating circles it is charitable to characterise the utter codswallop that your counterpart is foisting upon you as rhetoric. This is a courtesy that your opponent will appreciate and return later in the negotiation.

> **"The subtle difference between rhetoric and utter codswallop depends only on the context. "**

In the less rarefied negotiation to which you will have to descend in order, for example, to convince a train company that the absence of a train is a sufficient reason for a ticket refund, it is advisable to call utter codswallop just that.

Rhetoric is word that has a wide number of applications and is an ideal weapon with which to put down any point you don't understand. For points that are too clever by half, we recommend 'sophistry' as the put down of choice. That said, the delight in these words is that they are all-purpose devices, suitable for traversing almost anything, as in "I'm bound to point out that what you've just said is pure rhetoric/sophistry/semantics." Thus, in time, the maturing bluffer will enjoy using the terms rhetoric, sophistry and semantics interchangeably without ever knowing exactly what any of them means.

15

5 Deploying Latin

Latin is a welcome visitor to any negotiation. It has been said to be even more valuable than coffee and pastries, although whoever said that has probably never encountered genuine Italian cappuccino accompanied by a warm apricot Danish.

With the possible exception of *Caveat Emptor* (let the buyer beware), which should perhaps be avoided when selling, all Latin is good Latin. The bluffer should introduce, without hesitation, whatever Latin maxim comes easily to hand. Since it is not really in the nature of Latin maxims to 'come easily to hand' and since you are likely to need at least one, you should pack some. We would encourage active use of: *Res Ipsa Loquitor* and *Quad Erat Demonstratum*

> **❝Since it is not really in the nature of Latin maxims to 'come easily to hand' and since you are likely to need at least one, you should pack some.❞**

Use the above freely whenever you wish to say 'That proves my point' or 'Aha, gotcha' even though they mean nothing of the sort.

6 Point scoring

Despite the obsession with point scoring, negotiation is nothing like tennis. In fact it is probably the antithesis of tennis. Tennis requires great skill and agility; a lack of ability means you will be exposed instantly; and you have to wear shorts.

In a negotiation, a degree of skill is undoubtedly valuable, but sheer bravado is a perfectly workable alternative; your adroitness as a bluffer will ensure you are not easily exposed; and it is highly unlikely that you would be asked to wear shorts. If this should happen you would, it is confidently assumed, negotiate the cut and the material.

7 Acting in good faith

You can choose to believe that your opponent will act in good faith and has every intention of doing a deal with you on sensible terms. You can equally choose to believe that your pet rabbit, Andrew, is the reincarnation of Joan of Arc.

> **A degree of skill is undoubtedly valuable, but sheer bravado is a perfectly workable alternative.**

Alternatively, you can allow yourself a moment of un-abandoned cynicism, and entertain the possibility that your opponent is, in fact, driven by wholly unworthy motives. This could prove more constructive.

8 Firing an early warning shot

It is immensely satisfying to fire an early warning shot at your opponent. Whether it is actually a good idea is another matter entirely. An early warning shot should consist in a short, non-specific rumination, such as:

17

'What sort of a way is that to start a meeting?'

'If you're going to be utterly disingenuous we won't get far.'

'Frankly, I am very disappointed.'

Never, in any circumstances, make your early warning shot relevant or, worse still, specific. The ultimate faux pas is any early statement that mentions how much you are prepared to pay.

9 Being defamatory

For a number of reasons that need not concern you, it is harder than you might think to be defamatory

66 It is harder than you might think to be defamatory in a negotiation. 99

in a negotiation. You should take this as reassurance rather than a challenge.

Audacity, which you should certainly attempt, is not defamation. Neither is rudeness, but there is one caveat: it may not have the desired effect. If you call your opponent 'an irritating viper with the negotiating finesse of Mussolini', he may well be flattered.

10 Grandstanding

If you can claim the attention of all around you for more than two minutes, without being interrupted, heckled or abused, you can boast (preferable in the pub afterwards), that you 'owned the room'.

This is a subject that negotiators get disproportionately excited about. Seminars are given on 'finding your own power' and 'asserting control'. The important thing to know about 'grandstanding' is how to react to it. Generally, don't. 'Grandstanding' is a harmless and wholly meaningless pursuit, which is best ignored. If you must react, you could try: 'I'm sorry, but would you mind saying all that again?'

Learning

A point will be reached in the negotiation when all the initial pretence, posturing and filibustering is at an end. If, like many negotiators, you find that this is your strong suit, then it will be downhill from here on. You will probably have no idea when the time has come to stop posturing. No matter. If in doubt continue for a little longer.

> **If you can claim the attention of all around you for more than two minutes you can boast that you 'owned the room'.**

However, as with many things in life, such as when you are waiting in the wrong place for a taxi or when your boss dislikes you, sometimes you just know.

1 Finding the context

Negotiators like to stress the importance of understanding the full 'context' of a negotiation in order to comprehend the 'big picture'. As more of the context emerges through your careful probing, your opponent will find himself telling you things he would have preferred not to disclose. At this stage you should focus on the context itself and discount the spin that will inevitably emerge with it.

2 Listening

It will, by now, be apparent that the field of negotiation offers you lots of ammunition for conversational skills. When you opine, as you surely will, on your own breathtakingly dexterous technique, you can illustrate this by reference to the art of listening. You will explain that while less adept negotiators listen with their ears, you can listen with your mind, your eyes and, most of all, your heart. This sort of lofty twaddle plays particularly well in golfing and tennis circles.

> **Claiming to have read the core documents is dangerous, whereas you can assert, without fear of challenge, that you have 'read the room'.**

3 Reading

While claiming to be a multi-faceted listener, it does no harm to assert similar breadth in the area of reading. Claiming to have read the core documents is dangerous, whereas you can assert, without fear of challenge, that you have 'read the room'.

4 Making notes

You could be forgiven for thinking that you need to take some notes. This instinct is both correct and flawed. You need to take notes, but you must not. The rule is this: 'Bring notes but don't take notes.'

The sound negotiator is rarely, if ever, caught scribbling on a pad. Try to adopt a masterful approach to the entire subject of notes: take them along, assiduously refrain from consulting them and on no account make more until a deal is reached.

Doodling, on the other hand, is greatly to be encouraged. It demonstrates control, assurance and infinite peace of mind. Doodles should be collected at the end of the negotiation. Cartoons of your opponents with speech bubbles containing defamatory comments are

> **“Bring notes but don't take notes. Doodling, on the other hand, is greatly to be encouraged. It demonstrates infinite peace of mind. ”**

particularly valuable and must not be left behind. Nor any that reveal your hand as in the tale of two relatively senior lady lawyers who hosted a negotiation with an all male team of opponents. The ladies took an attractive young female assistant to sit between them at the negotiation. This had very little to do with her gaining experience and much more about creating a distraction. The ladies won the day handsomely. After the men had left, the ladies found a sketch which the visitors had carelessly left behind. There were no words, just a picture – of a rose between two thorns.

5 Delivering a lecture

You may find yourself attending a negotiation where you have a great deal you want to say. This might arise from your preparation or from your natural prolixity. You may even be tempted to deliver a carefully structured lecture. Avoid this temptation. Eighty percent of what you say in opening will be lost by the end of the negotiation. The skill is knowing how and when to deploy your best points. All at once is rarely best.

66In any combat sport it is sometimes necessary to yield a little ground. 99

A trickier conundrum is presented if, on arrival, you are the recipient of a short but compelling lecture to which there is no obvious answer. Anyone who has visited a Revenue office may empathise with this situation. In any combat sport it is sometimes necessary to yield a little ground. You can do no better than to take a lead from the skilful negotiator who had a well practised technique for this situation. He would listen calmly to every word of the stern lecture and then retort: "I agree with everything you have just said. If I was sitting where you are, I would have said the same thing. That is why I've brought you a proposal…"

6 Muddying the waters

Both sides should end the learning phase with a clear picture. This means that your opponent (if he is halfway competent) will understand the context, appreciate your needs and have an awareness of what is important to you. Whether this is desirable is a more complex question entirely. For this reason you may decide it is time to introduce some element of vagueness or outright confusion.

> 66 You may decide it is time to introduce some element of vagueness or outright confusion. This is known as muddying the waters. 99

If done deliberately this is known as 'muddying the waters'. By the time they clear, you may have formulated a new strategy.

A MUDDLE

In so far as negotiations have any coherent pattern, which they mostly don't, you can expect events to proceed to a mid point. The tone may change, a sense of business may be felt and a new common focus may be shared. Ideally this will be accompanied by a tingle of nervous excitement, or at least a fresh pot of tea.

Managing objections

Even the most quiescent negotiator will, at some point, have to say something. Whether this is something of substance is open to debate.

> **Listening and appraising are more valuable than talking.**

You will have appreciated that listening and appraising are more valuable than talking. You will also be mindful that information is to be traded not given away. So your policy, when it comes to talking, should generally be to confine yourself to:

a Initial pleasantries and rapport building (both strictly optional).

b Asserting values (if you have any, otherwise just point out that where you are 'coming from' is a 'good place').

c Asking open-ended questions.

These guidelines, implausible as it may sound, hold the key to our study of managing objections. Remember them.

It is hard to say which is the more fundamental element of a negotiation, managing objections or bidding. Happily no one will ask you. All you need to remember is this; when the time comes to manage objections you should regard it as an excellent moment to switch off your 'auto pilot' and give the proceedings your full concentration.

1 Recognising an objection

You cannot overcome a deeply rooted objection unless you recognise it. Try to think of spotting an objection as 'recognising an implied need' (unless articulated by a computer programmer, in which case it would be 'recognising an implied nerd').

A price objection is pretty easy to spot but, sadly, not as easy to approach as an 'implied need'. Nonetheless, the line to take with a price objection is that you have not established sufficient benefits – yet. In sales circles, the adage is this:

'Price is only an objection if they don't really want it.'

2 Overcoming an objection

The art of overcoming objections is half the negotiation. The other half consists of catering, posturing and showmanship. At a simple level (which will be more than adequate for the bluffer's purposes) the majority of awkward points will consist of smug observations and spurious assertions of fact.

> **❝The line to take with a price objection is that you have not established sufficient benefits – yet. ❞**

Such hurdles can be gleefully overcome by deployment of the excellent 'bluffer's all purpose pushbacks'. There are three of these and, as the strategic bluffer would expect, they all involve the word 'traversing':

25

a **Traversing the old**

If your opponent repeats a point that you had no idea how to deal with the last time, dismiss it as repetitious or passé. If you are feeling really pompous (and you can congratulate yourself for that), say: 'I wasn't taken with that point when you made it before and it doesn't improve with repetition.'

b **Traversing the new**

If your opponent conjures up a brand new point, reject it as an 'afterthought'. Again, happily, there is a pompous way of saying this; call it a 'recently invented theory'.

c **Traversing the rest**

If your opponent says almost anything else to advance his argument, be quick to point out that it is 'self-serving' (as though that were a bad thing) and then be ready to fall back on the reliable old favourite 'You would say that, wouldn't you.' There is no answer to that.

3 Conceding the trivial

In order to secure a bargain in which you get what is important and concede what is trivial, it helps immeasurably if you can distinguish one from the other.

The best negotiators will create a lengthy squabble about a trivial point, with every intention of conceding it. By contrast, many novice bluffers fall into the trap of conceding the trivial far too easily, often without getting anything in exchange. There are several good reasons why you should not do this and they are:

> **66** To get what is important and concede what is trivial, it helps immeasurably if you can distinguish one from the other. **99**

a   To your opponent the point may not be trivial.
b   It is fundamentally bad practice.
c   Your opponent may recognise it as bad practice, which can cost you some credibility.

4 Side-stepping the significant

There are really only two options available to deal with a serious objection – pretend it isn't there, or deal with it.

a   **Pretend it isn't there**

The feasibility of this strategy depends on the calibre of your opponent (which is a pleasant change, since most strategies depend on your own). If your opponent is remotely switched on and has managed to articulate a material objection, your chances of deflecting this by striking up a conversation about factory farming are slim. Offering to go out and buy a round of cappuccinos is probably a better move and even if it doesn't succeed, at least you will get a coffee, a pastry and a breath of fresh air.

b **Deal with it**

'Dealing with' things is easier than it sounds. It may sound counter-intuitive to the novice bluffer to actually 'deal with' anything, but help is at hand. The way to 'deal with' pretty much anything is to ask lots of questions.

> ❝ Your most valued ally is now the open-ended question – one so framed that it cannot be answered by a 'yes' or 'no'. ❞

Your most valued ally is the open-ended question – one so framed that it cannot be answered by a 'yes' or 'no' – i.e., any question starting with 'what', why', 'where' 'how' or 'when'. Cherish these words, take them to every negotiation and use them liberally.

If possible, try to link one of those invaluable little words to your opponent's needs, such as:

'Why is that important to you?'
'How strongly do you feel about that?'
'What are your priorities?'

Then, as if by magic, the objection will resolve itself.

If you can achieve this you should no longer regard yourself as a bluffer but as an accomplished heavyweight negotiator. Such mastery takes about a week. In time you will feel that all your hard work is paying off. You will sense that valueless items are being cleverly traded and that objections are being overcome. You will imagine that you can see light at the end of the tunnel. You could be right. Or it could be a freight train.

Coping with unpleasant moments

You can never entirely be prepared for someone hiccuping loudly, the sudden disintegration of your calculator into tiny pieces or a key participant falling asleep. The general axiom for dealing with uncomfortable moments is to ignore them. But be prepared for:

1 Long pauses

In ascending order of scariness, having no idea what to say next is the least of the perils the novice may encounter. Nothing comes more naturally to the amateur negotiator than coming to a complete standstill. Happily 'the pause' is a perfectly acceptable play. Senior negotiators will deploy

> **Happily 'the pause' is a perfectly acceptable play.**

'the pause' for effect. You may do it because you have absolutely no idea what to say or do next. The effect is the same, so long as you can carry it off with style. The style with which you should carry it off, by the way, is 'calm assurance'.

In a negotiation, when anything scary happens, the best reaction is always no reaction at all. Master this and you will have the most cherished weapon in the negotiator's armoury – the Poker Face.

2 Smoking guns

It is the abiding ambition of every prosecution lawyer to discover a nugget of evidence in the middle of a trial. These sorts of theatrics are sadly all too rare, but when they do happen, they endear the lawyer to the entire court room.

> **When anything scary happens, the best reaction is always no reaction at all.**

The same thing can happen in a negotiation. Sometimes a piece of information emerges which instantly undermines your entire bargaining position. It might transpire that the car you are selling is stolen or the position for which you are interviewing requires fluent Gaelic. Devastating developments are, not surprisingly, known as smoking guns. Not all are as dramatic as a still smoking pistol, but they have one thing in common. They always arise without warning (not that any warning would help). If your opponent finds the proverbial 'smoking gun', your negotiation aims will vaporise and your credibility will be in tatters. This can be disappointing.

30

3 Bullying

It is hard to negotiate when you are not thinking rationally and it is hard to think rationally when you are under pressure. This seemingly obvious phenomenon explains why negotiators attempt to intimidate each other.

The old hand negotiator would never tolerate bullying and neither must you. Like any kind of dance, negotiation requires two parties who understand the moves and respect the conventional boundaries. If your feet are being trodden upon, get off the dance floor.

> **The pure therapeutic value of an unrestrained paroxysm cannot be over-estimated.**

There is an adage, popular among negotiators, that holds: 'Don't get angry; get what you want.' But suppose you want to get angry? In that event, you should. Don't attempt to restrain yourself. It is true that your tantrum is unlikely to move a hair on your opponent's head (and you must be equally indifferent if he has a minor convulsion). On the other hand, the pure therapeutic value of an unrestrained paroxysm cannot be over-estimated.

> **There is an adage, popular among negotiators, that holds: 'Don't get angry; get what you want.'**

4 Loss of position

As things unfold you may get the uneasy impression

that your opponent has gained the upper hand. This is because negotiation works in the following way. From the outset, both sides race each other to try to reach the higher ground. The first one to arrive will stay there, never to be displaced. Meanwhile, over time, the other party will realise that this particular 'two horse race' has ended some while ago and that first place has already been claimed.

This is a sinister development that cannot go unchecked. In order to assess what has gone wrong, it is advisable to call a temporary halt or create an interesting diversion. In all probability the problem has arisen because:

❝ At times like this negotiators tend, reach for nautical metaphors. ❞

a you have allowed yourself to be cast in the role of persuader; and

b you are making a bit of a pig's ear of it.

At times like this negotiators tend, for some unfathomable reason, to reach for nautical metaphors. Your presentation is said to be 'holed below the water', and steps must be taken to 'keep the ship afloat' but you must first 'stem the tide'. Attempt to do this by saying something like:

'I am not comfortable with where this is going.'
'I am not sure where you are coming from.'
'I am not as green as I am cabbage looking.'

These are known as 'momentum stoppers'. Treasure them.

The seasoned bluffer finding the high ground lost in the race to the top, will realise and do something about it fast. The trick then is to deploy a 'role swapping strategy' (albeit this is less exciting than the name suggests) by making your opponent justify his position to you. The starting point is to be resolutely undecided. Think it, feel it, but don't actually say it; it will sound creepy.

> **The trick is to deploy a 'role swapping strategy' by making your opponent justify his position to you.**

By regaining the position of the controller your opponent is now the one to do all the encouraging, while your only contribution is to sit in judgement.

The sophisticated bluffer will always reposition so as to adopt the role of the undecided party in any scenario, thus:

Scenario	Conventional position	Re-positioned as
Selling	Do you want to buy it?	Convince me why I should sell it to you.
Price	Would you pay x?	Why should I sell it to you at that price?
Job	Will you hire me?	Why would I want to work here?

Be justly proud of this strategy, even if you can't

actually pull it off. Just attempting it is hugely commendable and shows promise of future advancement in the field. Be prepared to brag about this shamelessly to colleagues, through the acceptable medium of 'coaching'. The following will be particularly impressive, as a summary of your maxim: It is more important to own the decision than to own the room.

> **66 It is more important to own the decision than to own the room. 99**

It is the undecided party who owns the decision.

Indulging in mind games

It may be a little disconcerting to the bluffer to know that all negotiators, even those of the most modest stature, regard themselves as being adept at mind games. However, like any game at which one can be proficient without any training or ability, this should hold no fears.

1 Thinking

Remember: the most important head to get into is your own. For this reason, thinking during a negotiation is regarded as being worthwhile. This will present you as calm, measured and, of course, thoughtful. The fledgling negotiator will also be comforted to know that this is entirely acceptable behaviour, to which your opponent cannot object. On the contrary, if you announce that you intend to think about the situation (obviously for an unspecified period of time) your counterpart may proffer further information – or may even make a better offer.

> **Thinking during a negotiation will present you as calm, measured and, of course, thoughtful.**

The other significant advantage of taking a moment to think is that you might actually have an idea. If you elect to share this idea with your opponent, point out that it arose from 'thinking outside the box'. This will be important, particularly if it later transpires that the idea was harebrained.

2 Assessing the opponent's position

It has been said, by a skilled negotiator, that effective negotiating involves listening carefully and interpreting what you hear so as to assess the real interests of your opponent. Those who coach in this area believe that this calls for the development of

> **If your opponent repeats anything it is probably because he is fibbing.**

sophisticated communication techniques. What exactly these techniques are is not your concern. It suffices to know that if your opponent repeats anything it is probably because he is fibbing. For example, if he announces, at regular intervals, 'I may walk out at any moment' but is still present long after dark, you can assume that you are facing a mediocre bluff (and a mediocre bluffer).

> **'No' can mean 'Maybe' or even 'Yes'. On the other hand, it is fairly safe to assume that the seventeenth 'No' means 'No'.**

A different (but equally proficient) negotiator once explained how to interpret the word 'No'. He counselled, correctly, that 'No' can mean 'Maybe' or even 'Yes'. On the other hand, he added, it is fairly safe to assume that the seventeenth 'No' means 'No'. Therefore, while listening out for your opponent's interests, you should also try to gauge his sincerity. Moreover, since your opponent will be assessing your personal authenticity, bear in mind the following adage: Be sincere in everything and if you can't be sincere, then fake it.

3 Assessing your own performance

As the negotiation progresses you may be curious to know how it is going. Put such curiosity firmly to one side. The objective, in the heat of a negotiation, is not to concern yourself with how well you are doing.

There will be a perplexing array of styles and strategies on show. Rather than commit yourself to a deep understanding of these techniques, be content to know that if things feel like they are going well, then they probably are. Either that or you are being manipulated outrageously by your opponent.

4 Vocal tone and body language

The assessment of non-verbal signals is a vital weapon in the armoury of the advanced negotiator. Those who practise this dark art know, to the precise percentage point, what proportion of communication is non-verbal. It is always an impressively high percentage on which, oddly, none of them can quite agree. You should insist that it is 62%, irrespective of whether anyone actually asks you.

This murky business involves trying to assess what your opponent is thinking by watching parts of their anatomy. If his eyebrows define the southern coast of Norway, the game is up. If he leans back, scratches one ear and makes a noise not unlike a tractor, you are on the home straight.

> **If he leans back, scratches one ear and makes a noise not unlike a tractor, you are on the home straight.**

Analysing signals of this sort will offer the bluffer immense opportunities for amusement and distraction. Over time, you can build up a veritable glossary of interpretations of tone and gesture signals. Then, as well as assessing your opponent, you can indulge in transmitting some meaningless but intriguing gestures and sounds of your own.

5 Using N.L.P.

Even the novice negotiator should make full use of the techniques of Neuro Linguistic Programming (which you will always refer to as N.L.P.). Some would say that N.L.P. is no more than a fashionable label for assessing vocal tone. As a devotee and practitioner of the stratagem, you are not among those sceptics.

The theory of N.L.P. is that everyone falls into one of three categories: 'Auditory', 'Visual' or 'Kinaesthetic'. It follows that you must be one of these but, happily, you don't have to work out which one. The idea is to guess, from his behaviour, which one your opponent is, then pretend to be one yourself. This technique is known as matching (a good word) and enables you to connect (a very good word) with your counterpart. This is how to do it:

With Auditory people: Say 'I hear what you say'.

With Visual people: Say 'I see where you're coming from'.

With Kinaesthetic people: Say 'I sense what you're feeling'.

If you can manage to use these hackneyed phrases without looking sincere, you will be making great strides

N.L.P. at its simplest involves simply repeating what your counterpart has just said. An accomplished salesman tells of how he called a potential customer at a bad time. The customer said:

'You know what, I'm really busy right now, but you can give me a tinkle next week,'

to which the salesman duly replied:

'You know what, if you're really busy right now, I'm going to give you a tinkle next week'.

You might think that the customer would object to this blatant mimicry but, on the contrary, he assumed it was someone talking his language.

6 Visualisation

The concept of visualisation is, happily, the last of the 'Mind Games' to which we shall refer. Although it is by far the silliest, you can still speak highly of it among your peers. Just do not engage in it.

The idea is this. In addition to listening to your opponent, assessing vocal tone, reading body language and attempting mimicry, you must also get inside your own mind, assess what's in there, and then replace it with something different.

> **You must also get inside your own mind, assess what's in there, and then replace it.**

The sporting world is to blame for this nonsense. Before a contest, athletes visualise themselves winning a race, golfers visualise themselves holing out and football players visualise themselves in the pub.

Bidding

The meaningful part of any negotiation is the bidding. If all is well you will proceed smoothly along the bidding path without being tripped up by unresolved objections. Indeed, if your ground work has been done properly, you will be able to take these strides with great confidence.

> **66 The proper attitude to eye-wateringly outrageous demands is, of course, one of respect. In all matters of negotiation, being rational is strictly optional. 99**

We should add that, although abhorrent to all negotiators, it is possible to have a discussion where both sides do no bidding. Instead they assert values, secure positions and score points without either side ever formulating a coherent proposal. Master practitioners of this craft are known as politicians. Negotiators also prepare and posture, but always for a purpose, to lead, at some point, to a proposal.

1 Absurd demands

A well-respected protocol holds that before parties

commence making cynically unrealistic bids, they should first table their demands. The proper attitude to eye-wateringly outrageous demands is, of course, one of respect. In all matters of negotiation, being rational is strictly optional.

2 Derisory offers

There is a well-established tradition of discarding the first offer, whatever it is. Once the first offer and instant rebuff are out of the way, the sport can begin in earnest. Making an utterly pitiful offer can destabilise the negotiation, disrupt the flow and put the entire process in jeopardy. These are all good reasons for doing it. In due time, the furore will die down and you may make a slightly less contemptible bid. In the context of your previous pathetic offering, it may seem remarkably generous.

> **❝ Making an utterly pitiful offer can destabilise the negotiation, disrupt the flow and put the entire process in jeopardy. These are all good reasons for doing it. ❞**

We observe without emotion that there is a place for all manner of disgraceful behaviour in a negotiation. The art is to pick the right moment. As a general guide, a thoroughly despicable opponent deserves an equally despicable bid.

3 Promises and threats

As the negotiation gathers natural momentum you

may tire of advancing value-based propositions and asserting benefits. If your counterpart seems a little unreceptive, or even coy, you might try intimidation as an alternative approach. There are many ways of menacing your opponent politely and it is generally worth adhering to this convention. Many an otherwise effective bluff has been undone by want of subtlety.

> **It more than suffices to allude to a disadvantage or a potential problem that might lie in store. Threatening is all a question of degree.**

It more than suffices to allude to a disadvantage or a potential problem that might lie in store. Threatening is all a question of degree:

Enough	Too much
There are other interested parties.	Hurry up or I'll sell to someone else.
I'm not sure we are making progress.	Sign now or I'm leaving.
I'm disappointed.	I know where you live.

Strictly speaking, the rule is that you should not threaten to do something that you are not prepared to do. Junior to intermediate level bluffers are allowed some dispensation in this regard. Advanced bluffers can ignore it altogether.

4 Bluffs

It is worth mentioning that a negotiation can take place between two parties in all candour, without any gamesmanship, skulduggery or bluffing. It can, but it rarely does.

The complete absence of deception, or at least modest trickery, might unnerve some veteran negotiators. The traditionalist would regard a negotiation as incomplete (and wholly unsatisfying) if it did not contain at least one outrageous subterfuge. The question is, how to do it.

The technique for bluffing, is the same as for any other bid. You must deploy audacity and calm in equal measure. So, for example, in the case of a

> **66 For a breathtakingly outrageous bid, you should be breathtakingly and outrageously composed. 99**

moderately insulting bid, you should be moderately calm. On the other hand, for a breathtakingly outrageous bid you should be breathtakingly and outrageously composed. Sit back, make eye contact, speak clearly in a monotone and wear an expressionless face. If your opponent recoils a little you can assume that you have slightly overdone it.

The technique for double and triple bluffing is the same but, sadly, the opportunities arise less frequently. A bluffer's anecdote has it that two parties in an antique shop were bargaining over a Victorian salt cellar in the shape of Josephine, an ugly artefact that had been gathering dust in the shop for years. The shop owner expressed reluctance to part with it, an obvious bluff, but the buyer had the matching pepper pot, in the shape of Napoleon. To him the Josephine salt cellar had what negotiators excitedly refer to as 'marriage value'. The buyer pointed out, correctly, that the Josephine salt cellar was worth very little and that she was not, in all honesty, an attractive piece.

> **Negotiation has much in common with other endurance based contests, such as marathon running, Mahler or marriage.**

This game of bluff and double bluff went on until the shopkeeper guessed that only someone who owned the matching pepper pot would be remotely interested in such an article. The customer duly bought the pottery and paid more than it was worth (which was not difficult) because he was out bluffed.

Injecting a well timed bluff into a negotiation is equally useful when fielding an awkward question. For example, if you are asked 'What do you know about the thermodynamic expansion properties of this product?' any of the following would constitute a fine response:

"They are excellent."

"Everything there is to know."

"Enough to know we shouldn't get bogged down in that."

AN END

Negotiation has much in common with other endurance based contests, such as marathon running, Mahler or marriage. One such shared characteristic is the need for persistence even though no end is in sight.

Accepting Surrender

As the meaningful part of the negotiation emerges, so do the 'guiding truths'. One highly successful negotiator verbalised his guiding truth as: 'All I want is more.' This kind of sentiment has a clear meaning. In negotiation parlance, it means that there is a smell of business in the air.

> **As the meaningful part of the negotiation emerges, so do the 'guiding truths'.**

1 Managing the negotiation

As things hot up, even the most ambitious apprentice may struggle to manage all aspects of the negotiation simultaneously. With all the tea, coffee and mineral water that attends these events, the beginner should be more than satisfied with managing his own bladder.

Even at the business end of highly stressful negotiations, it is vital to give the impression that you can 'stay centred'. This can be a tall order, especially if you have no idea what 'staying centred' means. In essence it means 'remaining focused' which, roughly translated, means 'paying attention'. Negotiators prefer to say 'staying centred'. It sounds so much more professional.

2 Paying attention

The naïve negotiator would doubtless consider it to be axiomatic that you must pay attention throughout. Yet, it is surprising how many seasoned practitioners take a different view. Many would think nothing of negotiating by telephone while simultaneously completing Sudoku puzzles. Conference calls the world over are plagued by this kind of multi-tasking and it is particularly acute where time zones are involved.

"It is surprising how many seasoned practitioners would think nothing of negotiating by telephone while simultaneously completing Sudoku puzzles."

It may be early morning in Japan and the local negotiator may be in an air-conditioned office feeling energised for the day ahead. But what if his counterpart is at home in Coventry, it is 11.30 at night and the pubs have just closed? In these circumstances the best you can hope for is that the weary British negotiator contributes the occasional noise. If that noise is not obviously attributable to the consumption of alcohol, so much the better.

3 Losing the will to live

The negotiator's elation at securing the bargain of
the century will be concealed in an instant, like a
chocolate bar in a duffle coat. This is because the
competent bluffer will be able to hide many things
and most emotions. The negotiator's demeanour
will not give the slightest clue to an opponent that,
for example:

- The farm was repossessed last week.
- The star witness is in prison in Mexico.
- The head of the drilling team used to be a
  woman called Betty.

But there is one thing that even the very best
negotiators cannot conceal. Boredom. A world-
weary negotiator may try to sound focused, attempt
to look alert and pretend to be
engaged, but boredom will
seep out like damp through
wallpaper.

Demotivation is a fantastic
motivator. Fatigue saps the
resistance of the most robust

> **Fatigue saps the
> resistance of the most
> robust negotiator. In such
> circumstances any deal
> offers the prospect of
> something irresistible.**

negotiator. In such circumstances any deal offers
the prospect of something irresistible – the chance
to go home, and what would have been an unattrac-
tive offer a few hours earlier suddenly seems tanta-
lisingly good. For example:

11.30am

Offer: We propose moving the border 53 miles towards Chad and calling the new territory 'Harold'.

Reaction: Out of the question, we insist on making Chad bigger, not smaller.

4.45pm

Reaction: OK, well maybe you can have a bit of Chad but we insist, no more than five miles.

7.30pm

Reaction: Have as much of Chad as you want but you really can't call a new country 'Harold'.

11.15pm

Reaction: OK, enough, if everything else is agreed we can live with 'Harold'. My last bus goes in 10 minutes... are we done here?

4 Final offers

There is no such thing as a 'final offer', but that should not stop you making one and your opponent will certainly not feel deterred. It is an equally respectable option to label your offer 'non-negotiable' or 'final-final'. But not 'once and for all': it is too wordy, and doesn't have a hyphen.

As with everything in negotiation, ignore the adjectives and focus on the substance. Or, as negotiators like to say, listen and interpret. Final offers have to be dealt with. 'Dealing with' things, as the bluffer will recall, is accomplished by asking questions. A really splendid question to have up your sleeve is:

'What else is there we would need to talk about?' [not stated, but implicit '...to make you sign']

If you have the benefit of a client present, or any other kind of audience, you will later explain that this was your 'test close'.

Reaching agreement

It can be disconcerting when you have no idea what your opponent is thinking. If you find this disquieting, which you shouldn't, try visualising this: somewhere in your opponent's head is a donkey playing a ukulele. It might help, just a little. What would help a lot more would be a buying signal.

1 Recognising buying signals

A buying signal is any question from your opponent that implies, 'If the answer is correct, I will deal'. This is hugely exhilarating to negotiators. Not only does it give a clue about what the opponent is thinking (which would be valuable enough in itself), but it reveals that those thoughts are good thoughts, thoughts that can be worked with.

2 Blinking

As a negotiator you will have to occupy yourself when nothing much is happening, which can be most of the time. During a lengthy negotiation your activities may include drifting off or even nodding off. These are perfectly legitimate pastimes, provided you are still able to detect when your opponent 'blinks'.

> 66 During a lengthy negotiation your activities may include drifting off or even nodding off. 99

The expression comes from the analogy of a negotiation as a staring contest. The first one to 'blink' loses – so long as his opponent spots it, and acts decisively.

3 Biting an arm off

Negotiators have jargon for every scenario and plainly you must bandy about as much of this as you can muster. A highly significant (albeit rare) situation arises when your opponent makes an over-generous offer. The bluffer will accept such an offer after only the briefest pretence at hesitation.

The lexicon of jargon to describe this is limited to just one expression: 'I bit his arm off.'

4 Leaving money on the table

In the parlance of the assured negotiator (among whom you should be included), the process of negotiation is known as 'dividing the pie'. This means that everybody gets something and there is nothing left. Another neat way of saying exactly the same thing is to refer to a zero-sum game. Since it is always commendable to have a third way of expressing the same point, feel free to talk about the importance of not leaving any money on the table.

However, circumstances (usually adverse ones) may compel the negotiator to depart from this strategy. In the event of an absurd outcome it is often a good idea to point out that you deliberately 'left some money on the table'. Somehow, leaving money on the table will make sense even though it was a 'zero-sum game'. Indeed, this is an acceptable account of the outcome, provided always – and you must stress this – that it was done intentionally. Exactly why you would deliberately leave money on a table is a delicate question – but one that no-one will ask.

> **" In the event of an absurd outcome it is often a good idea to point out that you deliberately 'left some money on the table'. "**

5 Compromising

Conventional wisdom has it that negotiation is most effective when it is based on principles and values as opposed to simply maintaining a position. This is fine – in theory. Conventional wisdom, however, has less to say about giving up principles, values or even positions. This is because compromising is not a theoretical subject, it is a practical one. In practice, there has to be some compromise.

6 Closing

Those who negotiate in a sales context enthuse about the concept of 'closing'. This is because they don't enjoy negotiating, they enjoy selling. Closing is thus very important to sales people. It leads them from the dull part for which they don't get paid to the exciting part for which they do.

> **❝Closing is very important to sales people. It leads them from the dull part for which they don't get paid to the exciting part for which they do. ❞**

There are some people who find the act of negotiation to be its own reward. They will partake in it for hours upon end, sometimes with no apparent direction or conclusion. We call these people Italians.

All other negotiators will, at some point, face the salesman's challenge: how to end. There are two ways to close a negotiation and – be very clear about this – saying 'I rest my case' is not one of them. In all probability you will be hopelessly muddled about what your case is, let alone how to rest it. The two ways to close are these:

i **Qualifying the proposition**:
  Before conceding a point to your opponent, first obtain a commitment as to the consequences of the concession. This is known as 'qualifying the proposition'. For instance:
  Question: 'Does it come in green?'
  Answer: 'If it did would you buy one?'

ii **Accepting the proposition**:
  Accept the best deal available and summon a taxi.

7 Walking away

Walking away is not the end of the negotiation. It is an integral part of it. Whether you are negotiating in a Moroccan market to buy a donkey, or in a football club to buy a player (who may also turn out to be a donkey), you can always walk away. Moreover, you can do it several times. And if the unthinkable happens – you walk away and your counterpart does not pursue you – then you have learned something of great value: how far to push. Remember one thing about walking away. You can always go back. Always.

> **Whether you are negotiating in a Moroccan market to buy a donkey or in a football club to buy a player (who may also turn out to be a donkey), you can always walk away.**

There is no rule that every negotiation has to end in a deal. If it feels wrong, it probably is wrong. So don't do it. Take note of this story.

A small boy prayed for a new bicycle for Christmas and promised, in exchange, to be good. When the bicycle didn't materialise the child complained that God hadn't been listening. He was told that this was not so. God had listened to the proposition and the answer was 'no'.

In a negotiation you are God.
You can say no.

8 Deciding

Your initial goals in the negotiation, assuming you ever had any, may well have been forgotten by this stage. It is therefore worth emphasising that the objective of the negotiation is to determine one thing: what is the best deal available? Having established this, all that remains is to make a decision. This, unfortunately, can be the hardest part.

> 66 There is no rule that every negotiation has to end in a deal. If it feels wrong, it probably is wrong. So don't do it. 99

The time for bravery is over, which can be reassuring if you have so far failed to summon any. The attribute now required is decisiveness. If you need an insight at this pivotal moment, consider this Zen saying: 'In your heart, you already know.'

You own the decision.

Memorialising the deal

Many a naïve negotiator has been undone by lack of clarity in the final deal. A handshake or a clap on the back can be reassuring, but there is no substitute for a clearly written deal. Even in a simple case where goods change hands for money, many perils await the imprecise negotiator. Suppose, for example, your counterpart has promised you that in exchange for an agreed sum of money he will deliver to you all the goats he owns:

> **A handshake or a clap on the back can be reassuring, but there is no substitute for a clearly written deal.**

a   He may not own any goats.
b   He may have put all his goats in his wife's name.
c   The place of delivery may be unclear and while you're waiting in a field the goats are in your apartment eating your sofa.

NEGOTIATING STYLES

In most of life's activities, from driving to dancing, style is important. This is particularly true of negotiation. Style might be the only thing that a novice negotiator has and it's generally all that one needs.

> **Style might be the only thing that the novice negotiator has and it's generally all that one needs.**

There are rather too many styles to choose from, so we set out a selection, since the enthusiastic bluffer may want to master more than one. Such natural optimism is greatly to be encouraged.

As part of your preparation, you need to decide in advance how you feel about – or 'visualise' – your opposite number. This will inform whether you think of him as your 'Counterpart' or 'Opponent'. In this way you can be consistent (unlike this book, in which the terms are used interchangeably).

Your 'visualisation' (a great word – use it often) of the other party will depend on your own adopted style.

Your adopted style	You see the other party as
Combative, competitive.	An opponent.
Collaborative, enlightened.	A counterpart.
Untrained, naïve.	A benign uncle.
Taoist.	An ancestral spirit.

1 The marathon runner

If offered a choice between stamina and talent, opt for stamina every time. There are countless ways to exhibit stamina during a negotiation, but very few ways to display talent.

2 The village idiot

A valuable piece of Dorset wisdom holds: 'Never start an argument with an idiot, bystanders may not be able to tell which of you is which.' Unfortunately, if you are going to be a negotiator, starting arguments with idiots will be part of your daily ritual.

Certain commentators recommend playing dumb as a style of choice. Tempting as this may be, our firm advice to the bluffer is to allow your opponent to monopolise

> **66 Idiocy is, by common consensus, not a great attribute in a negotiator – or anyone else. 99**

this territory. Idiocy is, by common consensus, not a great attribute in a negotiator. If your opponent presents signs of profound stupidity the first thing to do is to assess if it is real or a bluff. There is no tactful way to do this, but do your best – your opponent might take offence if you ask him/her to write his name in the sand with a stick.

On the other hand, don't try to be too clever; you'll only complicate matters. A wise negotiator once gave the following analysis: 'If it has long floppy ears, a fluffy tail, and hops, it is probably a rabbit.' Sometimes, things are what they appear to be, even in the murky world of negotiation.

3 The uninformed purchaser

While stupidity has little intrinsic value, ignorance is greatly to be respected. The land of the unin-formed is always a good place for the bluffer to begin. There are three types of information-based bluffs, all of them legitimate.

a **Feigning expertise**: this strategy, in which you pretend to be comprehensively informed about the subject matter, is so common among negotia-tors as to be trite. It is a simple and amusing bluff that depends on the (usually safe) assump-tion that your opponent doesn't know enough about it to ask a difficult question.

b **Feigning ignorance**: a subtle and enormously satisfying bluff, which, in all probability, you will never pull off. Plainly that should not deter you from trying. The trick is as simple as it is elusive and involves:
  • Firstly, gaining a vast and agile knowledge of a (preferably complex) subject.
  • Secondly, admitting to finding the subject

beyond you and inviting your opponent to assist you with his greater intellect. This will be an irresistible proposition for any negotiator.

- Thirdly, listening earnestly to whatever contrived piffle your opponent tries to foist upon you – a ruse that allows you to take occasional sport in seeking elaboration and picking out inconsistencies.

This technique will help you establish the integrity of your opponent in the most satisfying way. If he is being misleading you'll know it and, better still, he won't know that you know it. Sometimes a step along the way is more important than the destination. Here is a case in point. The ability to engineer one of these 'I know but my opponent doesn't know that I know' situations is a moment of the utmost fulfilment. The canny negotiator who has achieved this will leave the negotiation purring with contentment, irrespective of the actual outcome.

> **Sometimes a step along the way is more important than the destination.**

c **Admitting genuine ignorance**: this strategy has an element of truth to it but that should not deter a bluffer. It is counter-intuitive to admit lack of knowledge and preparation, but there is a good deal to be said for this approach as it forces your opponent to try to 'sell you' on whatever the idea might be. And, as you have already established, the negotiator in the role of 'buyer' who gets the opposition to act as the 'persuader' will then own the decision. Good lines to take are:

- 'You'll have to excuse my ignorance.'
- 'I am happy for you to explain it to me.'
- 'I am open to persuasion.'

4 The relationship builder

The aim of the relationship builder is to foster good, long-term relationships. If you adopt this style you will regard the relationship itself as one of the desired outcomes, and will set out to find common values and create synergies. You will, at the same time, identify yourself as a deplorable sycophant of the worst kind. Of all the unconscionable and scurrilous negotiating styles to be encountered, the relationship builders garner the least admiration from their peers.

5 The co-operator

This is dangerous territory. Adopting a co-operative negotiation style commits you to actually working with your counterpart, who you are obviously not now allowed to call your opponent. The whole bogus idea is to try to find a mutually satisfactory solution. If you are a rank amateur and your counterpart is a sophisticated negotiator, or a more experienced bluffer, you will be led gently to a solution. But in the cold light of day it will be revealed as highly unfavourable to you, and all the more galling because of your active role in creating it.

By all means use the language of co-operation. Say things like 'Work with me on this' and 'Let's explore that together'. But, as with everything else in the shadowy world of negotiation, remember not to take yourself, or anything else, too literally.

> 66 Charm is usually an adequate substitute for talent, although never in the same league as persistence, which trumps everything. 99

6 The charmer

In the field of negotiation, as in life, charm will get you a long way. It is usually an adequate substitute for talent, although never in the same league as persistence, which trumps everything. When deployed as a negotiating device, charm will manifest itself by a warm demeanour, sincere vocal tones and open body language. This will enable your opponent to feel a sense of rapport as you fleece him.

The charming negotiator will entertain everything but agree nothing. The style commits one to listen intently, consider all ideas and welcome any suggestions. A shorthand term to describe this approach is to 'yes them to death'.

7 The persuader

It can be liberating to adopt the role of persuader. Like taking the lead in a bicycle race, it requires stamina, conviction, balance, and some sense of direction.

Of course there are significant perils to this approach. You might contradict yourself, lose your opponent's interest, or come to a complete and exhausted standstill. None of these events should alarm you overly.

> **A moment of grandiose show-boating followed by an inept silence is all part of the everyday rough and tumble of your new life as a negotiator.**

A moment of grandiose show-boating followed by an inept silence is all part of the everyday rough and tumble of your new life as a negotiator. Just try to give the impression, at all times, that you are entirely content with whatever you have just said or done. Then, in the metaphor of the bicycle race, get back on your bike and carry on pedalling.

The persuader is a stranger to doubt and will avoid cautious sentiments, such as 'you can never be sure' or 'correct me if I am wrong'. Strive to maintain an air of disarming confidence in everything you say. After all, you're only negotiating, not assessing the size of the hole in the ozone layer.

8 The win–win method

This is spectacularly simple. Through a process of understanding your counterpart's needs and priorities you craft a bargain which leaves everyone satisfied. If you can create an opportunity to brag about this miraculous feat (something you will obviously try to do) describe it as the 'loaves and fishes' technique. You may also get to be the next secretary-general of the UN.

9 The win–lose exponent

This technique can be summarised as:

> 'I want everything I want. I also want everything you want, irrespective of its value to me.'

This 'give me everything' approach will inform your strategy from the outset. It requires that you:
- find out what there is to be had;
- demand all of it, and
- never compromise.

It is good manners to signal to your opponent, at the outset, that you are a win–lose practitioner. One cunning negotiator habitually set in the middle of the table a plate of biscuits. As his counterpart was taking a seat the veteran would pull the plate towards himself, just out of the other's reach. The signal was clear: I am in control here and one prize has already escaped you.

10 The bare knuckle fighter

The win–lose approach works particularly well when harnessed to a style sometimes referred to as 'bare knuckle'. The visual image is of a burly street fighter, bloodied but unbowed, willing to trade blows (but nothing else) until his opponent gives up.

66 One cunning negotiator habitually set in the middle of the table a plate of biscuits. 99

Banish any thoughts of affability. If you are going to deploy this method, there is no point starting with a pleasant demeanour, it will only confuse your opponent when he asks you for the correct time and you respond by questioning his parentage.

11 The closed book

Like any closed book you will be unreadable. No clues will be given away by what you say (not much), how you dress (unremarkably), or how you react (you don't). Your opponent will have no idea what you are thinking, which, at times, might be very little. This will give you many advantages. Your opponent will be troubled to distraction that he doesn't know what to make of you. And if you don't know what you are going to do next, it won't matter a jot because your opponent won't know either.

12 The sheep in sheep's clothing

There is a large body of authoritative written work on the difference, in negotiating terms, between:

The Wolf in Sheep's Clothing
The Sheep in Wolf's Clothing
The Wolf in Wolf's Clothing
The Sheep in Sheep's Clothing

Playing any of these roles can involve strategies and sub-strategies befitting each type, with splendid scope for confusion. Sadly this pastime is not for the novice negotiator. We consider it to be hard enough remembering if you're buying or selling, without trying to decide what kind of animals you and your opponent might be. However intriguing this subject may appear, the apprentice bluffer is advised to give it a wide berth.

It will suffice the bluffer to remember only this gem. A sheep in sheep's clothing is, when all is said and done, a sheep. Having so decided, you will find that several things follow:

a Your opponent, who would prefer to be outside eating grass, knows even less than you do about pretty much everything, not least how to negotiate.

b You can start low. There is no opening bid which is so silly that it will do more harm than good. By the way, you should refer to outrageously silly opening bids as 'low ball' offers.

c Since most sheep can't actually bid, you will probably have to bid against yourself.

13 The untrained expert

Lack of research, experience and insight has never stopped the journeyman negotiator from pontificating if the need arises. Neither should it stop the bluffer. The technique is comfortingly simple. Talk at length and with confidence for as long as you can carry it off. End your homily by introducing a new subject, the inference being that you have opined definitively on the previous one.

> **Start low. There is no opening bid which is so silly that it will do more harm than good.**

This sort of legitimate padding must be distinguished from the less palatable phenomenon of the 'untrained expert', who will not only wax on commandingly and without any substantive foundation (which is, of course, perfectly acceptable), he will also seek to fortify his remarks by asserting that they are based on the highest available authority – himself. Those who succumb to this unworthy ploy will say things like:

'Trust me, this is my field.'

'I wouldn't say it if it wasn't true.'

'I lecture on this subject; I think I know what I'm talking about.'

14 The stuck record

The simplest example of asserting positions (rather than values) is the repetition – which is a feature of most divorce battles – of 'I want the house'.

This is the 'Stuck Record' method of negotiation, which consists of going in armed with no more than three things to say and repeating them ad nause-am. The technique is not without value because your counterpart will:

a eventually become convinced that you will not be shaken from the stated position; or

b lose the will to live.

Certain things are worth repeating for the sake of being repetitive, even though they don't mean much. Again, these remarks should, ideally, be 'values' to which you 'appeal'. Examples would be:

'We should all be tolerant.'

'There must be some give and take.'

'We all need to be mindful of ethical considerations.'

'Culture Club were vastly over-rated.'

15 The impersonator

An interesting conundrum arises when your counterpart has a 'negotiating style' and you don't. You
may have other things, such as an expensive wrist-
watch, high cheek bones or a deep appreciation of
the early works of Bob Dylan.
These are covetable assets but
they will not compensate for
your complete lack of any kind
of negotiating style.

Eccentricity alone would not be a reason to dismiss a strategy and it works surprisingly well.

The imbalance is easily
remedied. You simply copy your opponent. This is
not as eccentric as it sounds (although eccentricity
alone would not be a reason to dismiss a strategy)
and it works surprisingly well.

16 The Taoist

The beauty of the Taoist approach is that it
harnesses Eastern philosophy to the modern commercial milieu. And if you can say that with any
degree of conviction your opponent will be ravaged.

The Taoist sentiment is:
> 'It is what it is.'

The bargaining theory is:
> 'The meaningful process takes place in the mind of the party being persuaded.'

Put them together and you get:
> 'Persuade me, tell me what it is'.

It is possible to obtain a Taoist disposition, but not everyone can spot that you have one. It is not enough simply to adopt a Taoist demeanour, you must make everyone aware of it (even though this is a very un-Taoist thing to do).

Your demeanour	**How you announce it**
You are open to persuasion.	Say this at the outset, calmly.
You view everything objectively.	Say this as well, regularly.
You have an open mind.	Say this when you're cornered.
You are willing to abide by the outcome.	Say this to devastating effect.

Before you can say Tao Te Ching (which you probably shouldn't) you own the decision.

NEGOTIATING SCENARIOS

Encountering negotiating scenarios is not a problem, they are everywhere. The trick is recognising them and then succeeding in the ensuing combat.

1 Face to face

Your opponent may or may not be facing you. Likewise he may or may not be listening to you. There are many permutations but the most common is the opponent who is facing you but not listening to you. All these permutations are types of negotiation. Leaving a cryptic voicemail is an act of 'negotiation' just as spending three days in a tent with an assortment of Middle Eastern leaders. On the other hand, leaving a voicemail will not get you any air miles.

> **Leaving a cryptic voicemail is an act of 'negotiation' just as much as spending three days in a tent with an assortment of Middle Eastern leaders.**

2 Remote

The idea of remoteness should not be taken to extremes. If you wish to contribute to a negotiation, it is generally considered that turning up is a sound starting point.

Although your absence may send a powerful message, it is harder to influence an outcome if you are not actually there. This is a statement of the obvious, which is a technique to which you should become firmly wedded.

3 Buying and selling

Buying is considered to be a sophisticated art although, in fairness, many negotiators have untrained spouses who are naturally adept at it. Anyone whose job title includes the word 'purchasing' will confirm to you that buying is a hugely challenging business which requires complex processes. How else, for example, would the professional purchaser know how to prioritise all the corporate entertainment invitations?

> **66 This is a statement of the obvious, which is a technique to which you should become firmly wedded. 99**

When approaching such a vast subject the bluffer should always have, readily to hand, a sweepingly controversial statement. Whether it is true (or even arguable) is of far less consequence.

In the context of buying and selling, there is only one sweepingly controversial statement worth having. It is this: 'There is no such thing as selling, there is only deciding to buy.'

4 At work

The world of work contains a series of daily negotiations involving different levels of subtlety. The exception is dealing with unions, which involve none. Collective bargaining, as it is known, is a contest between the company, which employs specialist negotiators, and the union, which employs amateurs. The union usually wins.

5 Resolving disputes

Always be prepared to assert that you can negotiate anything, that no subject matter is beyond your ability as a negotiator to confront and deliver an outcome that is at once stunning and audacious. In the event that you actually achieve this (as opposed to predicting it) you are entitled to refer to the resulting deal as 'sweet' or 'first rate'. 'Legendary' may be a little flowery.

66 Be prepared to assert that you can negotiate anything, that no subject matter is beyond your ability as a negotiator. 99

Your assumed expertise is such that you must regard the idea of outside help as absurd. Judges, mediators and arbitrators are examples of the sort of external influence that you should particularly try to avoid. These individuals are your predators. If they cannot be avoided they should be handled with the utmost caution.

If anyone suggests that such an agency is needed

to help resolve a complex dispute, you must try to stamp it out. Assert that it would be utterly super-fluous in view of your prodigious skills in the area. It is not that there is no room for an ill-informed, interfering outsider. There is, but that is *your* job.

6 Mediations

It doesn't hurt to know the difference between a mediator and an arbitrator although, truth be told, it doesn't help much either. A good line to trot out to anyone who doesn't know is this: unlike an arbitrator or a judge, a mediator does not decide the outcome of a dispute; he helps the parties decide it for themselves. Facilitator is a good word to toss in should the opportunity arise.

> **It is not that there is no room for an ill-informed, interfering outsider. There is, but that is *your* job.**

If you have to deal with mediators, there are some pretty safe rules to follow:

i **Be firm and fearless**. Whatever they try to tell you, sell you, talk you into or out of, stand your ground. Realising that something has to give and that it is not going to be you, the medi-ator will turn his fire on your opponent.

ii **Be relentlessly polite**. A mediator will see any sign of discourtesy as progress.

73

iii **Be patient**. Most mediators get paid by the day, so mediations always take a full day, at least. The first four hours are entirely occupied by posturing and the next four by bullying.

You have been warned.

7 Agents

If you are given the honour of negotiating with someone else's money, the convention is to recite the 'Agent's Oath' which states: 'I will negotiate on your behalf as though this were my own money.' Estate agents rarely make this promise.

It is advisable to bear in mind that your role as agent should involve not one but three negotiations:

i **Before battle**. If you fail to recognise the huge significance of expectation management, your life expectancy as an agent could be measurable in hours. Negotiate with your principal to establish your authority limits. Setting his expectations relatively low is a good move.

ii **In battle**. Negotiate with your opponent. To 'close' you can use the agent's mantra: 'If you want to do something today, that's as far as I have authority to go.'

iii **Post mortem**. Negotiate with your own principal again.

8 Multi-party negotiations

Multi-party negotiations offer a safe hiding place for the amateur negotiator. Imagine that you are one of several parties battling feverishly over a complex issue. Imagine, furthermore, that the others all understand the subject better than you do (in all probability they will not, they will just be more experienced bluffers). Suppose that the others are all trading blows and scoring points, except you. This can be daunting. But remember: if you're there it is probably because the others cannot consummate a deal without you. Relax, smile benignly, and frown every eight to ten minutes. At some point someone will tell you what has been going on – assuming that they know. If you don't like the sound of it, announce your displeasure in earnest terms and go home.

> **Remember: if you're there it is probably because others cannot consummate a deal without you.**

When multi-party negotiations end in this chaotic fashion, which most of them do, you should be remorseless. Have at your disposal an appropriate description to account for the outcome. We would recommend 'It was a bridge too far', or the trendier equivalent 'It cratered'. We tend to discourage 'It ended in abject disarray' because this implies an element of blame, which should at all costs be avoided.

9 International negotiations

Never argue with a German when you are tired.

10 Begging

Begging is undoubtedly a negotiation scenario, albeit rarely recognised as such. Convention has it that the beggar goes first and opens with 'Spare some change for a cup of tea Guv?' You duly part with some cash and the beggar, in the best Dickensian tradition, says 'Gawd bless you, Guv.' You do not get to speak.

> **Convention has it that the beggar goes first and opens with 'Spare some change for a cup of tea Guv?'**

This has all the ingredients of a successful negotiation. The beggar gives you information as to the goods in question, you form a view on how much you are prepared to pay, a bargain is struck and both parties are satisfied. True, the beggar gets the cup of tea, not you, but you get the beggar's blessing and a warm glow of self-satisfaction.

11 Borrowing

In contrast to begging, borrowing is often regarded as a more complicated transaction. This is odd because the similarities between begging and borrowing are overwhelming. There is a short discussion, you hand over something of value and you never see it again. Only the warm glow is missing.

12 Mugging

The primary advantage of mugging, as a negotiating scenario, is that it doesn't take long. You would therefore do well not to invest too much time devising a complex counter-strategy. Rather, you should endeavour to make your best point succinctly. Signs of a successful negotiation with a mugger are that you still have your bus fare home and are not bleeding profusely. If you still have any means of telling the time, you have done particularly well.

"If you are pleased with the outcome, never say so."

The mugging scenario highlights another key technique of the proficient negotiator. If you are pleased with the outcome, never say so. At the conclusion of a mugging you would not, for example, announce: 'It's a relief that you don't like music or you might have stolen my iPod.'

13 Dating

The process of courtship is not analogous to a negotiation, it is one. All the obvious ingredients are there: selling, buying and expensive food. The less obvious elements are also present: listening, interpreting and shameless insincerity. Then there is 'closing'. Closing is a delicate and complicated subject at the best of times. In the context of dating, however, the question of closing does not need to be discussed here.

14 Spouses

It is easy to fail to spot a negotiating scenario, but easier still to convince yourself that you are negotiating when any fool could see that you are not. Many husbands, for example, like to imagine that they are negotiating with their wives when, on a proper analysis, they are merely receiving instructions.

15 Children and other forms of terrorist

It is an essential truth that you cannot negotiate with a child or a traffic warden, but for very different reasons. One is immature, sulky and irrational while the other is only a child. Negotiation is a mutual process. It requires two parties capable of reasoned thought to commence the negotiation. Thereafter, to procure the desired outcome, it also helps to have something with which to bargain.

> **Many husbands, like to imagine that they are negotiating with their wives when, on a proper analysis, they are merely receiving instructions.**

The notion of bargaining chips is metaphorical. We are not speaking here of French fries, except in the case of children, where it works about as well as anything else.

Securing a bargain in theory, without being able to enforce it in practice, is a classic journeyman's error, which will amuse your opponent immeasurably. In any negotiation where your counterpart is your own teenage offspring, you can expect to be taken for everything you have promised and at least 30% more. In return, the teenager will not only fail to deliver his or her part of the bargain, but will deny having promised to do so and accuse you, quite correctly, of being delusional.

16 Inanimate objects

Your assumed omnipotence as a negotiator should extend to inanimate objects. Assert, preferably with a straight face, that scientific research has now established that inanimate objects can be cajoled into life whereas threatening them is utterly futile. Foul and abusive language will elicit a response, but, invariably, not the one desired.

> **❝In any negotiation where your counterpart is your own teenage offspring, you can expect to be taken for everything you have promised and at least 30% more.❞**

Be prepared to recommend a more measured negotiating strategy. Advise that the best tack is to try reasoning calmly with the machine. If that fails, point out that the negotiation with the device is at an end. It is now acceptable to hit it with a blunt object.

17 Lunch

It is a myth that 'anyone can be bought'. It is unlikely, for example, that the Dalai Lama can be bought. That said, if this were a serious proposition, there are certain plucky negotiators who would fancy their chances of delivering His Holiness.

The proposition could safely be re-worded as 'any waiter can be bought'. The negotiation with a waiter is simple. You provide cash in exchange for which your lunch goes well. Given the vital importance of lunch to negotiators, this should never be forgotten.

THE POST MORTEM

Bluffers at all levels should take the opportunity of a post mortem. The history of the negotiation may disclose many salient details. It is your job, as chief historian, to ensure that the record is set the way you want it – favourably. Of all the potential outcomes, failure to consummate can be the trickiest to excuse.

Even successful negotiations merit some degree of retrospection, as exemplified by the tale of the two wealthy negotiators sitting in the First Class Eurostar lounge in Paris. They reflected on another successful jaunt and in the spirit of honest reflection (which we would cautiously recommend), one said to the other: 'At least we're only morally bankrupt.'

Your reasons for doing a post mortem will vary, depending upon the outcome of the negotiation.

1 Justification

A common problem with negotiation is having to justify the outcome to someone else. As we've already stressed, this is also a great negotiating tool since it arms you with the stock response: 'I couldn't justify that...'

The person to whom you must justify your decision may be an employer, a client or a spouse. Theoretically you would also have to justify it to yourself, but this kind of critical introspection is to be avoided.

> **The appropriate tactic is often to put a really positive gloss on the outcome, however catastrophic it may be.**

In a negotiation the primary tactic, obviously, is not to get hopelessly out-manoeuvred and reach a ludicrously one-sided bargain. Should this go wrong, the appropriate tactic is often to put a really positive gloss on the outcome, however catastrophic it may be. If asked to explain, for example, to the Queen why you have given away the Duchy of Cornwall in exchange for a set of saucepans, it will not suffice to say that it seemed like a good idea at the time.

2 Exculpatory statements

The sophisticated negotiator will have a strategy, readily to hand, for the 'follow up negotiation', which will take place with those to whom one is accountable. Some of the following may assist:

> 'I pushed them as hard as I could.'
>
> 'I didn't want to jeopardise the deal.'
>
> 'My primary goal was to preserve some goodwill in the relationship.'
>
> 'If you think that's bad, you should've seen their first offer.'

3 Celebrating

In America the expression 'getting pissed' means getting very angry during a negotiation. In Britain it means getting very tipsy.

66 If you can't celebrate the outcome you can still celebrate the conclusion. 99

There is a time for composed dignity and a time for smugness and self-satisfaction. Remember that the former is for all stages up to and including saying goodbye. The latter is for the remainder of the week.

Wherever you are in the world, whatever sort of negotiation you have just concluded and (most importantly) whatever the outcome, always find a way to celebrate. If you can't celebrate the outcome because, say, it was an unmitigated calamity, you can still celebrate the conclusion. The fact that a negotiation is over justifies a degree of natural exuberance.

If the muse takes you, stand at the airport in the manner of Neville Chamberlain, holding aloft a piece of paper. If you are not lucky enough to be quite so self deluded, then find a way to celebrate that makes sense to you. Take a moment. Sit in a park. Drink some tea.

> **❝ The fact that a negotiation is over justifies a degree of natural exuberance. ❞**

GLOSSARY

Ad nauseam   Sickening TV commercial.

Arbitrator   Hired gun whose exorbitant fees are paid, in advance, by two parties equally. Upon payment, the Arbitrator will release a written decision as to which party has been shot.

Belt and braces   Two clauses in a negotiated settlement that say exactly the same thing.

Boilerplate   Numerous (well, at least four) pages of wholly impenetrable standard clauses placed, at some expense, into a settlement.

Conspiracy theory Implausible explanation offered by others and immediately discounted by you, to account for events for which you have no better explanation.

Dividing the pie Slicing a pastry before adorning with cream. This forms part of an important study topic which expert negotiators call 'lunch'.

Drill down Term used by senior negotiators to describe the detailed research they genuinely intended to do.

Dynamic Term used to describe either (a) the complex inter-relationships within any group or (b) yourself.

GTXM Encouragement to opponents: Go the extra mile.

Hardball An inflexible negotiating style that can descend to shouting, adopting a purple pallor and table thumping. Others present will appreciate this amusing spectacle. The table may not.

Heads of terms Manuscript note written, at the eleventh hour, to misrepresent the outcome of the previous 10 hours' negotiation.

Leverage Subtle but consistent force, used to unlock a bargain (or a champagne bottle).

Low ball   A shamefully small offer made to upset your opponent or test his sanity.

Maybe   Probably not.

Making notes   Singing quietly to yourself in moments of acute stress, boredom, etc.

Mediation   Three-way tussle involving two parties with opposing ambitions on either side of a third who is utterly indifferent.

Meeting craft   Behaviour, however irrational, aimed at controlling a group.

No   Maybe.

No brainer   All purpose justification for any seemingly inexplicable decision. So called because no brain was involved in making it.

Perspective   Your opponent's view of life which, however strange, sometimes appears real to him.

Ratify   To become increasingly ratty.

Reading   Desirable key preparation stage. If omitted say: 'I don't need to read the documents when I can read the room.'

Remorse   A melancholic sensation, unknown to negotiators.

Role play   Fiddling nervously with bread.

Slam dunk   Insertion of ice into tall glass as precursor to assembling vodka and tonic.

Specious   Bullshit.
Spurious   Utter bullshit.

Subject to contract   Maybe.

Sumo   Jotting, sometimes seen on opponent's notepads. Means 'Shut up, move on'.

Sweetener   Small item, thrown into a deal or a warm beverage.

Tactics   Said to be different from strategy. No-one can explain how.

T&Cs   Terms and Conditions or, for the more enlightened, teas and coffees.

Unintentional consequences, Law of   Useful panacea, can excuse a multitude of sins.

U.S.P.   Characteristic falsely ascribed by sales people to every proposition.

V.A.T.   Vodka and tonic.

V.F.M   Value for money. A good concept to raise in the face of price resistance.

Yes   Maybe.

THE AUTHOR

Alex Geisler lives in London, a small town near Bournemouth. He is a frustrated bus driver. If successful in his career of choice, he would have spent his working life negotiating the narrow streets of Dorset on a number 13 bus. Fate decided otherwise and he now negotiates complex engineering disputes instead, as a partner of an international law firm.

He continues to believe that his family will support his wish to adopt a life of leisure, but has found himself hopelessly outmatched in this negotiation.

The loves of his life are, in no particular order: one perfectly ancient green bus called Fluffy, one perfectly horrid grey cat called Moodles, two perfectly outrageous daughters called Stephanie and Olivia, 11 imperfectly formed footballers called AFC Bournemouth, and one perfectly formed wife called Joanne.

Economics

So-called invisible earnings arise from income earned from abroad by the service sector. A word of warning though: make sure you remember where you put it down or you'll have a devil of a job finding it again.

Flight Deck

If the weather is fine, enthusiastic pilots often disengage the autopilot in the latter stages of the descent and fly the aircraft by hand. Not only is it enjoyable, but with the relentless increase in automation it is sometimes a comfort to discover they still can.

Consulting

Never underplay your hand. It is important to remember that everyone knows and expects consultancy to be an expensive business. Nobody should be disillusioned in this matter. It is always a good plan to invoice expenses separately from fees. This has the benefit of seeming to reduce the overall total.

Management

The secret of good management is avoiding bad management. Similarly, the test of good managers is that they cannot be observed or remembered for the deviations and idiosyncrasies which make bad managers so memorable.

Philosophy

Of course, any sensible theory is neither one thing nor the other; and it's generally safe to say something to that effect without fear of having to say just how much of one, or the exact proportion of the other.

Opera

It is fairly safe to make up bits of an opera plot as nobody is likely to challenge its validity. A fair number of them are just as intelligible after reading the synopsis as before. The whole point in having opera mainly in a foreign language is that the plot can be totally ignored.

Small Business:
"Accessible and amusing, this book manages to deliver some superb advice. Categorising it in the humour section is daft, as it deserves to be ranked along with the classic business texts."
Reader from Bristol

Teaching:
"Teaching told like it is. So many of the observations of situations are exactly right! Essential reading for every parent and should be on the recommended reading list at all teacher training colleges."
Reader from Scotland

Philosophy:
"Extremely funny yet surprisingly informative. A real treat for anyone interested in philosophy."
Reader from Jerusalem

Accountancy
"This book worked wonders on my tax returns. With the skills I had learned here I was able to bluff my way through the yearly records in merely half-an-hour."
Reader from West Midlands

the Bluffer's® Guides

Accountancy	....	The Olympics	....
Archaeology	....	Opera	....
Astrology	....	Paris	....
Banking	....	Philosophy*	....
Bond*	....	Psychology*	....
The Classics	....	Public Speaking*	....
Consultancy	....	The Quantum	
Cricket	....	Universe*	....
Doctors	....	Relationships	....
Economics	....	Rocket Science*	....
The Flight Deck	....	Rugby	....
Football	....	Seduction	....
Genetics	....	Sex	....
Golf	....	The Simpsons	....
Hiking	....	Skiing	....
Jazz	....	Small Business	....
Life Coaching*	....	Stocks & Shares	....
Management*	....	Surfing	....
Marketing	....	Teaching	....
Men	....	University	....
Middle Age	....	Whisky	....
Music	....	Wine	....
Negotiation*	....	Women	....

Oval Books

*This Bluffer's® Guide is available
as a downloadable audiobook:
www.audible.co.uk/bluffers

We like to hear from our readers.
Please send us your views on our books
and we will publish them as appropriate on
our web site: ovalbooks.com.

Oval Books also publish the best-selling
Xenophobe's® Guide series –
see www.ovalbooks.com

Both series can be bought via Amazon or directly
from us, Oval Books through our web site
www.ovalbooks.com or by contacting us.

Oval Books charges the full cover price
for its books (because they're worth it) and
£2.00 for postage and packing on the first
book. Buy a second book or more and postage
and packing will be entirely FREE.

To order by post please fill out the accompanying
order form and send to:
Oval Books
5 St John's Buildings
Canterbury Crescent
London SW9 7QH

cheques should be made payable to: Oval Books

or phone us on +44 (0)20 7733 8585
or visit our web site at: www.ovalbooks.com

Payment may be made by Visa or Mastercard and orders are
dispatched as soon as the card details and mailing address are
received. If the mailing address is not the same as the card holder's
address it is necessary to give both.

Oval Books